Peep!

MathStart®
UNDERSTANDING CAPACITY

A HOUSE FOR BIRDIE

by Stuart J. Murphy · illustrated by Edward Miller

HarperCollinsPublishers

LEVEL 1

To Michael and John—
who, like Birdie's friends, have
made our house perfect for us
—S.J.M.

To Lucien Wostenholme
—E.M.

The publisher and author would like to thank teachers Patricia Chase, Phyllis Goldman, and
Patrick Hopfensperger for their help in making the math in MathStart just right for kids.

HarperCollins®, 🏠®, and MathStart® are registered trademarks of HarperCollins Publishers. For
more information about the MathStart series, write to HarperCollins Children's Books, 1350 Avenue
of the Americas, New York, NY 10019, or visit our website at www.mathstartbooks.com.

Bugs incorporated in the MathStart series design were painted by Jon Buller.

A House for Birdie
Text copyright © 2004 by Stuart J. Murphy
Illustrations copyright © 2004 by Edward Miller III
Manufactured in China by South China Printing Company Ltd. All rights reserved.

Library of Congress Cataloging-in-Publication Data
Murphy, Stuart J.
    A house for Birdie / by Stuart J. Murphy ; illustrated by Edward Miller.—1st ed.
        p.   cm.—(MathStart)
    [Understanding capacity, level 1].
    Summary: As Birdie and his friends try to locate a house that is just right for his size, readers learn about the
concept of capacity.
    ISBN 0-06-052351-4 — ISBN 0-06-052353-0 (pbk.) ✓
    1. Volume (Cubic content)—Juvenile literature. 2. Size perception—Juvenile literature. [1. Volume (Cubic content)
2. Size perception.] I. Miller, Edward, ill. II. Title. III. Series.
QA465 .M854 2004
530.8—dc21
                                                                                            2002152615

Typography by Edward Miller   1 2 3 4 5 6 7 8 9 10   ❖   First Edition

A House for Birdie

Poor tiny Birdie had no house. When the rain fell, he got wet. When the wind blew, he was always cold.

One day, Birdie gathered his friends together.

Spike was tall, thin, and narrow.

Queenie was tall, fat, and wide.

Goldie was short, fat, and wide.

And Fidget was short, thin, and narrow.

"I need a house," peeped Birdie. "Can you help me find one that's just the right size for me?"

Peep!

Off they all flew to find a house for Birdie.

"Look, there's a nice house in that tree," cawed Spike.

"It looks way too tall for me," peeped Birdie.

9

Birdie was right. It was tall, thin, and narrow—just like Spike.

"It fits me better than my old house," cawed Spike. "I think I'll move in."

Queenie, Goldie, and Fidget followed Birdie as she flew on.
"There's a pretty house on that pole," honked Queenie.
"It's much too fat and wide for me," peeped Birdie.

They all looked at the house. Goldie tried to get in.

"I can fit," she squawked. "I'm fat and wide."

"No way," honked Queenie. "You're much too short. It fits me the best and I could use a new house. I think I'll take it."

15

Goldie, Fidget, and Birdie kept going.

"Over there on the fence," squawked Goldie. "There's a cute house."

"It's short like me, but it's very fat and wide," peeped Birdie.

SQUAWK, SQUAWK!

"I can fit," chirped Fidget.
"But it's much too fat and wide for you," squawked Goldie. She climbed in and it was perfect for her.
"I think I'll stay," squawked Goldie.

19

That left Fidget to help Birdie
find a house.

"I'll never find a house that's
just right for me," peeped Birdie.

Peep!

"Wait," chirped Fidget. "There's a lovely house on that limb—and it's very short and narrow."

"Well, it might work," peeped Birdie hopefully.

Birdie tried it out. "It may be short and narrow, but it's still too big for me," she peeped.

"We'll it's nice and thin, too," chirped Fidget, "just like me."

"There's no house that's the right size for me," peeped Birdie sadly.

It started to rain. The wind began to blow.

Birdie was wet and cold.

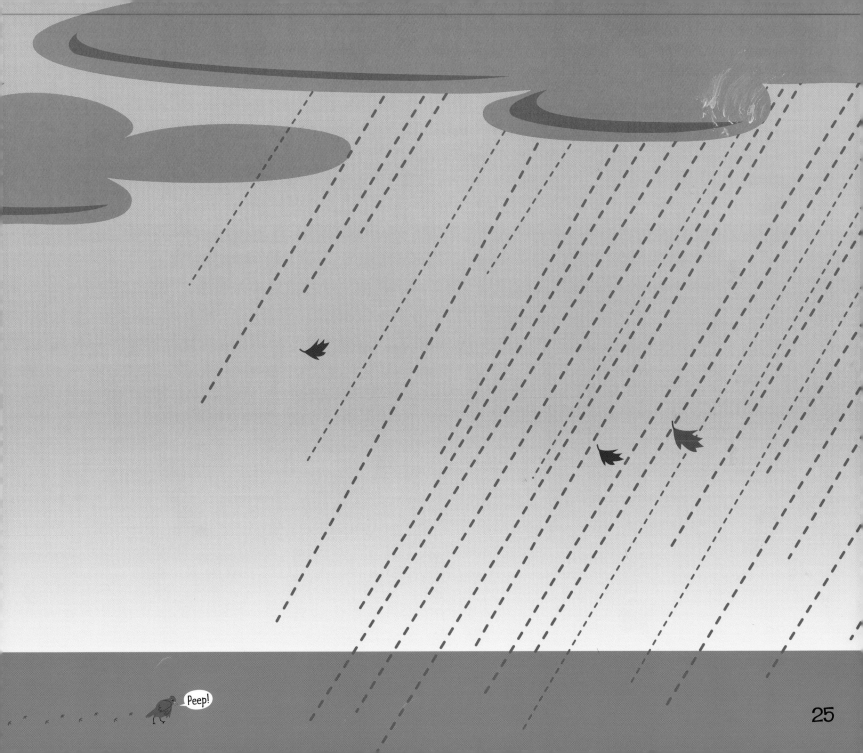

"Oh, no!" cawed Spike.

"How awful!" honked Queenie.

"This is terrible!" squawked Goldie.

"We must do something!" chirped Fidget.

And they all flew over to help Birdie.

Peep!

So Spike gathered some twigs.
Queenie picked some leaves.
Goldie found some grass.
And Fidget put it all together.

Birdie was dry and warm.
"This house is tiny all around!"
peeped Birdie. "It's just
the right size for me!"

Peep,
peep!

FOR
ADULTS AND KIDS

In *A House for Birdie*, the math concept is capacity, or volume. Capacity is the measurement of how much a three-dimensional shape can hold. Seeing the relationship between a shape's dimensions (length, width, and height) and the quantity it can hold is an important step in a child's understanding of capacity.

- Read the story to the child and encourage him or her to describe the attributes of each bird. Using the same words as those in the story, discuss how these attributes match those of each bird's chosen house.

- Imagine the child is a bird. Have him or her describe his or her own shape and then draw a picture of a birdhouse that matches the shape. Choose other members of the child's family and have the child draw birdhouses that would fit their shapes.

- Choose three or four of the child's stuffed animals. Have the child decide which is taller, which is thinner, and which is wider. Then select appropriately sized boxes and have the child decide which animal fits best in which box.

- Have the child blow up three different size balloons. Discuss the size of each balloon. Which one was the hardest to blow up? Why?

- When mailing a package, have the child help choose the best size box from four or five empty ones.

Following are some activities that will help you extend the concepts presented in *A House for Birdie* into a child's everyday life:

PET STORE: Visit a pet store that sells birds. Help the child match the different birds to the birdcages that would make the best fit.

HOW MANY CUPS?: Give the child a 1-cup measure and a few larger containers. Ask him or her to guess how many cups of water are needed to fill one of the larger containers. Have the child check the estimate by filling up the container, one cup at a time. Continue with the other containers.

BUILD A TOY BOX: You will need tape, scissors, cardboard, and two or three of the child's favorite toys. The toys should be of different sizes. Precut appropriately sized pieces of cardboard. Help the child pick the correct pieces of cardboard to tape together in order to make a box for each toy.

The following books include some of the same concepts that are presented in *A House for Birdie*:

ANNO'S MATH GAMES II by Mitsumasa Anno
WHEN THIS BOX IS FULL by Patricia Lillie
MATH COUNTS: *CAPACITY* by Henry Pluckrose

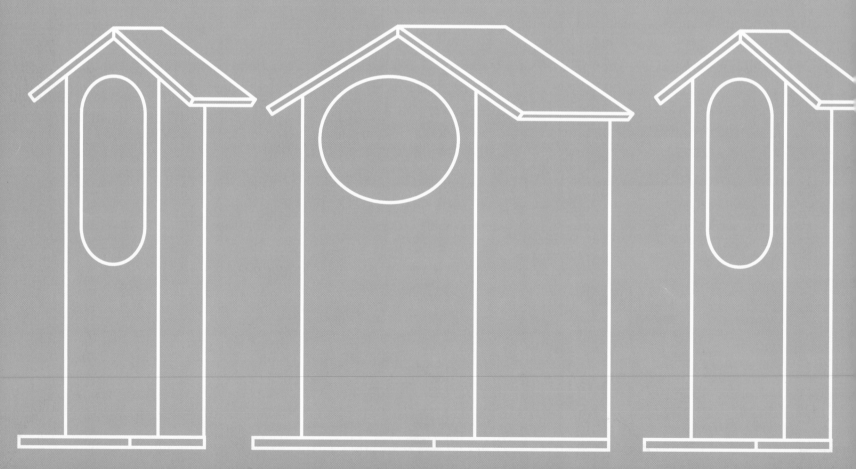

Peep!